Wonderful Words

Edited By Lynsey Evans

First published in Great Britain in 2024 by:

Young Writers
Remus House
Coltsfoot Drive
Peterborough
PE2 9BF
Telephone: 01733 890066
Website: www.youngwriters.co.uk

All Rights Reserved
Book Design by Ashley Janson
© Copyright Contributors 2024
Softback ISBN 978-1-83565-436-1
Printed and bound in the UK by BookPrintingUK
Website: www.bookprintinguk.com
YB0590I

FOREWORD

Welcome Reader, to a world of dreams.

For Young Writers' latest competition, we asked our writers to dig deep into their imagination and create a poem that paints a picture of what they dream of, whether it's a make-believe world full of wonder or their aspirations for the future.

The result is this collection of fantastic poetic verse that covers a whole host of different topics. Let your mind fly away with the fairies to explore the sweet joy of candy lands, join in with a game of fantasy football, or you may even catch a glimpse of a unicorn or another mythical creature. Beware though, because even dreamland has dark corners, so you may turn a page and walk into a nightmare!

Whereas the majority of our writers chose to stick to a free verse style, others gave themselves the challenge of other techniques such as acrostics and rhyming couplets.

Each piece in this collection shows the writers' dedication and imagination – we truly believe that seeing their work in print gives them a well-deserved boost of pride, and inspires them to keep writing, so we hope to see more of their work in the future!

CONTENTS

Al Mizan School, London

Hannah Noor (11)	1
Khadeejah Ryhan (10)	2
Ammaar Hasan (10)	4
Ubaidah Ahmed (11)	5
Yusuf Uddin (10)	6
Afrin Sharmin (11)	7
Rayhaan Abdur Rahman (10)	8
Zakariyya Abdul Wadud (10)	9
Muaaz Noor (11)	10
Tahmid Mohammed Razzak (11)	11
Tauheed Hassan (10)	12

Bradshaw Hall Primary School, Cheadle Hulme

Arinola Ogunkoya (9)	13
Yasmeen Yousef (10)	14
Alice Owens (10)	15
Hamza Hussain (10)	16
Melika Norouzi (10)	17
Maddie-Mai Mulholland (9)	18
Lois Glodkowski (9)	19

Braywood CE First School, Oakley Green

Astrid Grove (8)	20
Zedrick Morley Fretes (8)	22
Charles Roos (9)	23
Lyra Shiels (9)	24
Amarah Teymorian (9)	25
Orla Byrne (9)	26
Caden Cherry (8)	27
Noah Jones (8)	28

Lara-Jayne Kinane (8)	29
Alys Lancaster (9)	30
Mia Komal (8)	31
Kiran Uppal (9)	32
Humphrey Kinloch (8)	33
Sophia Mezzena Walker (9)	34
Jasmine Smallwood (10)	35
Dylen Thomas-Dibb (9)	36
Diya Narang (8)	37

Calshot Primary School, Great Barr

Belkys Nsiri (11)	38
Holly Stonehouse (11)	40
Aaliyah Heaven (11)	42
Ishpinder Kaur (11)	43
Harps Skye (11)	44
Juwairiyah Kazi (10)	45
Vimaljot Singh (9)	46

Clenchwarton Community Primary School, Clenchwarton

Skyla Freestone (9)	47
Esme Turner (8)	48
Martha Turner (8)	49
Isabella Wells (9)	50
Olivia Oczos (8)	51
Daniel Dolby (9)	52
Henry Neve (8)	53
Noah Ridge (8)	54
Grace Burrell (9)	55
Charlie Fisher (8)	56
Mia Meek (8)	57
Charlotte Chapman (8)	58

Harper Comley (8)	59
Megan Burch (9)	60
Evie Buckingham (9)	61
Bella Godfrey (8)	62
Alyssa Doy (8)	63

Gorseland Primary School, Martlesham Heath

Abigail Green (7)	64
Hoorain Syed (8)	65
Benjamin Maximo Armengol (8)	66
Brooke Holland (7)	67
Jacob Alam (7)	68
Olivia Pitt (8)	69

Hamilton College, Hamilton

Fathmah Abid (11)	70
Bella Babalola (11)	72
Kavata Velle (11)	73
Ben Psaila (11)	74
Caleb Browning (11)	75
Misha Shafiq (11)	76
Blair Kinnoch (11)	77
Shannon Olusola-Johnson (11)	78
Blaine Robson (11)	79
Rafe Chesworth (11)	80
Rebecca Coughlan (11)	81
Harris Cunningham Mason (11)	82
Kathleen Bullen (11)	83
Tafara Mutezo (11)	84
Ethan Akun (11)	85

Oak Tree Primary School, Mitcham

Unaysa Zakir (9)	86
Saarah Zahid (11)	87
Yusuf Usman (10)	88
Aisha Shahzad (10)	90

Perranporth Community Primary School, Liskey Hill

Elodie (7)	91
Ezra Law (7)	92
Freyja Ballinger (7)	94
Danny Williams (7)	95
Elsie Smith (7)	96
Maya O'Brien (7)	97
Emily Carter (7)	98
Noah Kershaw (7)	99
Pixie Griffiths Grant (8)	100
Rory Lane (7)	101
Amy Thomas (8)	102
Teddy Whiting (7)	103
Maisie Palmer (7)	104
Kirk Pietrasz (7)	105
Bonnie Ansell (8)	106
Lucas Chegwidden (7)	107
Taron Aldridge (7)	108
Isaac Thomas (8)	109
Indie Hurley (7)	110
Harry Webber (7)	111
Harmony Grant (7)	112
Levi Schick (7)	113

St Lawrence CE Primary School, Chobham

Amelie Callaway (10)	114
Skyla Bullock (7)	116
Jessica Cassini (9)	118
Emily Igoe (7)	119
Alexa Cooke (10)	120
Eve Lynch (9)	121
Sadie Field (11)	122
Jack Arnitt (10)	123
Darcy Toropov (8)	124
Abigail Draper (10)	125
Sinead Loveridge (9)	126
Emelia Stacey (8)	127
Freddie Hunt (9)	128
Nathan Cooke (9)	129
Marygrace De Cillis (9)	130

Rafe Newton (10)	131
Clarke Phelps (10)	132
Harper Hobson (8)	133
Cora Wilks (9)	134
Poppy Brown (7)	135
Olivia Hunter (9)	136
Odessa Newton (7)	137

St Mary's Primary School, Bathgate

Eden Storrie (11)	138
Amelia Christie (10)	140
Lilia Kay (10)	142
Gracie Shaw (10)	144
Kristiana Ramule (11)	145
Emily Marshall (10)	146
Erin Lumsden (11)	147
Haniya Shahzad (10)	148
James Greig	149
Ethan McGinty (11)	150
Roma Purdie	151

St Michael's Primary School, Newry

Ronan Carragher (7)	152
Mia Casey (8)	153
Neasa Carragher (8)	154
Sevda Greauvgiua (8)	155
Ruby McVerry (7)	156
Sophie Galbraith (7)	157
Nicole Hristova (8)	158
Lorcán Connolly (6)	159

Stockbridge Primary School, Edinburgh

Basil Ransom (10)	160
Elsa Brett (10)	161
Archie Roberts (10)	162
Freya Blathwayt (10)	163
Emir Karabacak (10)	164
Jasmine Spence (11)	165

Maria Coelho-Spanos (10)	166
Ghofran Almutbage (10)	167
Isla Gilchrist (11)	168
Elsie Douglas (10)	169
Thea McDougall (10)	170
Albie Dagless (10)	171
Petra Kyriakides (10)	172
Emile Henry-Davies (10)	173
Naya Alzoubi (10)	174
Andria Khupenia (10)	175
Noah Sherwin (11)	176
Billie Morton Giovacchini (10)	177
James Lim Young (10)	178
Diane Oreoluwa Afolabi-Fakunmoju (10)	179

Sutton Road Primary School, Mansfield

Kyle (8)	180
Freyja Wyatt (8)	181
Petros Murataj (9)	182

Willows Primary School, Grimsby

Teddy Butler (8)	183
Maxwell Leonard (7)	184
Emmanuel Ratubuli (7)	185
Amelia Kaminska (7)	186
Joshua Evans (7)	187
Lucas Cottard (7)	188
Alexander Williamson (7)	189

Woodmancote School, Woodmancote

Nancy Carter (9)	190
Verity-Iris Rowles (9)	191
Marley Williams (9)	192
Evie Kirchner (8)	193
Lily Robinson-Kirk (8)	194
Zoey Pervaiz (9)	195
Ariyah Anderson (9)	196
Ivy Graham (8)	197

Alice Fleming (9)	198
Lilly-May Dancey (9)	199
Grace Pearce (8)	200

THE POEMS

My Extraordinary Weird Daydreams

D reaming about black holes is one for a start!
A daydream that will make you ponder about the times you laughed
Y our worst fears of the dark will start to become true
D ream dust in the black hole will make you go achoo!
R aucous noises will fill your ear
E veryone in your grasp will slowly disappear...
A thought of loneliness shall come through your head
M ore of your dark thoughts will be imprinted on your hand with lead
S uddenly, within a blink of an eye, I come back to reality with a huge sigh.

Hannah Noor (11)
Al Mizan School, London

Space Explosion

As I fall asleep, this is what I see,
Galaxies, asteroids, comets, stars,
We jump into a rocket,
Heading for Mars.

We zoom through the air,
Stars shining bright,
Past the wonders of space,
All through the night.

Stars and meteors,
Shooting down,
Asteroids everywhere,
All around.

Suddenly, a ball of burning flame,
Smashes into our rocket,
The explosion that follows,
Is too bright to explain.

We fall down through the air,
Senses lost,
Am I here?
Or am I there?

An almighty crash,
A blinding flash,
We are alive,
But the rocket is now ash.

Khadeejah Ryhan (10)
Al Mizan School, London

The Abyss Of Betrayal

Groping around in the dark abyss,
Not a soul to be seen.
But a figure, oh so familiar,
Was I in a dream?

The friend that looked at me,
The friend that approached.
A strange glint in its eyes I could see,
As if it meant to coax.

I was so foolish, not a single clue,
Holding a hand that was sure to fade.
If only I realised, if only I knew,
Not a sense I'd been betrayed.

I opened my eyes; I was all alone,
The betrayer was gone.
I'd been betrayed, by now I knew,
I'd been toyed with all along.

Ammaar Hasan (10)
Al Mizan School, London

Starvation

A deadly raccoon going through the road,
Staying outside even though he's cold...
He never ever does what he's told...
If you cross his path you will feel his wrath,
He goes through your bins,
Looking for your tins,
He's treacherous, he's monstrous,
He has no morals at all!
If you ever encounter this deadly raccoon,
Just give him your bins and all of your food,
Because he is none other than the... deadly raccoon!

Ubaidah Ahmed (11)
Al Mizan School, London

Nightmare

N othing has prepared me for the dream.
I take a leap forward, as scared as I can.
G od knows what will happen; every step is insane.
H ow can I be here? I am trembling in fear.
T ing, oh no, what's that sound?
M onsters creep out from the ground.
A step back and the monster will get angry.
R umbling in fear, the monster disappeared.
E ver would I? Who knows if I will.

Yusuf Uddin (10)
Al Mizan School, London

Getting Lost

G etting lost is a pain
E verything is unknown
T ill this day I have not been found
T elephone calls have not come
I just want to disappear
N othing such as good luck has ever come
G etting lost is a pain

L onely feelings all day
O nly friend is the bird
S ometimes I think that I can be found
T ired sighs just occur away.

Afrin Sharmin (11)
Al Mizan School, London

The Shadow Knight

'T was the night, not a creature in sight,
H aunting shadow under the moonlight,
E verlasting dread in the night.

S ound is what you can't hear if he is near,
H ate to tell you, your end is here,
A nticipate his arrival,
D eath will come, beg for survival,
O pen your eyes, don't scream,
W ake up, it's a dream.

Rayhaan Abdur Rahman (10)
Al Mizan School, London

An Illusion

I n a pitch-black land,
L urking in the shadows is a shady man,
L ike a cheetah, he runs at me,
U pon his sprint, I realise he's my fear in the form of a being,
S hort of time, I close my eyes,
I n the distance, he approaches me,
O ver me, his shadow suddenly fades away because,
N ow I'm sitting up, eyes awake, in my bed.

Zakariyya Abdul Wadud (10)
Al Mizan School, London

In My Jungle

The tales of the jungle have begun,
The tales for all of creation,
A vibrant jungle with its mysteries,
A perfect place to give me the jeebies,
For in this place, traps lay around,
It'll stalk you for days and then surround,
Forgotten people and lost treasure,
Waterfalls and rivers to the eyes such a pleasure,
For this is my jungle,
But can you imagine yours?

Muaaz Noor (11)
Al Mizan School, London

Bilbo Baggins (Lord Of The Rings)

Bilbo Baggins, an inquisitive fellow,
Who once had a wonderful meadow.

Accompanied by thirteen men,
As powerful as the myth of Fen.

Fighting through the misty mountains,
Hoping to reach the heavens.

Ready to take Erebor,
To ultimately set the score.

Victory is a true tale,
Defeat is a piece of folklore.

Tahmid Mohammed Razzak (11)
Al Mizan School, London

Getting Lost

I woke up in a giant forest,
My friend Jack was surprised,
We were worried we were going to stay,
I ran and found a dead chicken,
I went back and he was missing,
I tried shouting but it didn't work,
I ran and ran and suddenly,
I found him inside a river.

Tauheed Hassan (10)
Al Mizan School, London

My Life

I'm all alone and I see the moon in the ebony sky
I wish I could just lay my head and listen to my mind
When I lay my head I dream of stars
And see when astronauts land on Mars
In life, there is a purpose to fulfil a destiny
I don't know what is mine but in the future we will see
Life is a roller coaster, it goes down and up
Like if you see someone sad say *cheer up*
We should appreciate everything we have because people might not have it
Even if you have a birthday gift and you really don't like it
So would you be invisible or do you want to be here?
But if you're happy please say a cheer!

Arinola Ogunkoya (9)
Bradshaw Hall Primary School, Cheadle Hulme

How Far Will Your Dream Take You?

My dream is a recommended holiday,
An ambition in your mind.
A series of thoughts and sensations,
A human can never find.

My dream is a magical adventure,
That you will always find in your brain.
Bursting with imagination and colour,
That you will always try to maintain.

My dream is a moment to behold,
Which will probably have changes and bends.
A spirit that will light up the way,
And will hopefully not come to an end.

Yasmeen Yousef (10)
Bradshaw Hall Primary School, Cheadle Hulme

Forever Football

From childhood dreams to the stadium lights,
I chase stars on moonlit nights.

In the heart of the game, I find my place,
And live the dream with my every chase.

From goal to goal, the battle unfolds,
In my football dream, triumph beholds.

Underneath the stadium skies,
The floodlights caught my eyes.

With every kick, ambitions rise,
With every goal, I feel the prize.

Alice Owens (10)
Bradshaw Hall Primary School, Cheadle Hulme

Imagination And Dreams

Have you ever had a bad dream?
Like when you let down your football team,
You look up and see their angry faces,
If they forgive you they show no traces.

Have you ever had a good dream?
Like getting an A+ in a test,
And everyone thinks you're the best,

Whatever dreams you have enjoy them,
Your imagination starts to tear because we get older every year.

Hamza Hussain (10)
Bradshaw Hall Primary School, Cheadle Hulme

Once Upon A Sky

The crystal sky is shining bright in my eyes,
The destiny that I want to be is the shadow,
Singing high like a unique bird being shy,
My imaginary mind is dreaming while sleeping in the night,
Like a bonfire on New Year's night,
Coming from the sky is a snowy day,
Light like a glowing sunshine at night,
That sets like the moonlight.

Melika Norouzi (10)
Bradshaw Hall Primary School, Cheadle Hulme

How Lucky I Am

In the morning I woke thinking how lucky I am
The shower is running
The smell of the breakfast downstairs
Warming up my clothes ready to wear
Not forgetting about my breakfast downstairs
Ready to eat whatever I've got
Because I don't mind whatever I've got
Not forgetting how lucky I am.

Maddie-Mai Mulholland (9)
Bradshaw Hall Primary School, Cheadle Hulme

Magical Midnight Island

As waterfall falls,
And tropical birds call, *squawk!*
While shooting stars fly,
In the purple and pink sky.
A dream is going to be mine.

Then, the bright blue ocean
Glimmered like a sapphire potion.
Shimmering in the sun,
Before midnight comes.

Lois Glodkowski (9)
Bradshaw Hall Primary School, Cheadle Hulme

When I Go To Bed

When I go to bed,
And rest my busy head,
I dream my house is red,
My name is Ted,
And my friend is Zed.

And on the second night,
I see a massive fight,
About a blazing light.

When I jump into my bed,
And rest my whirling, twirling head,
I look down at the ground,
And see that it is red.

The fight has killed my family,
And Zed is no longer with me,
Monsters roam around,
On the tormented ground.

I decide to blink,
And start to think,
With a wink,
The ground turns pink,
And I begin to think,

I feel a thump,
And my heart starts to pump,
I'm in my bed,
I raise my head,
I will never go back to bed.

Astrid Grove (8)
Braywood CE First School, Oakley Green

Harry Potter

Underneath the setting sun,
Is a castle, all to come,
As the train arrives,
All the students come to rise,
As a boy walks by,
For an almighty feast comes by,
Before we feast
The sorting hat comes out of hiding,
As I was put into Gryffindor,
We began to feast,
Bon Appetit,
Many years ago,
A cloaked figure still stands in front of Godric's Hollow,
Avada Kedavra,
Both of them fell,
As the boy lived his life,
Grief swallowed him inside,
But as he has his friends by his side,
He lived happily ever after,
Conquering his fears which stored him inside,
As he conquered darkness and grief,
He brings light all around.

Zedrick Morley Fretes (8)
Braywood CE First School, Oakley Green

An Ancient War

I wake up in my dream, lonely and scared,
But ready for a mighty fight,
All so energetically strong.

Suddenly a strand of my hair falls to the ground,
It turns into a bright purple lightsaber,
And there's a golden dragon to help me win the fight.

With all my might I start to fight,
My dragon roars as the rain starts to pour,
My saber sizzles with the light,
The sun shrinks by the fight,
At night we end the fight.

We become victorious,
With a flicker of a flame,
And we are not to blame for the fight,
We overcame,
Suddenly I woke up,
The day is shining bright, without a fright.

Charles Roos (9)
Braywood CE First School, Oakley Green

Dream World

Close your eyes,
Snuggle up tight,
Time to go to Dream World,
Look around,
It's beautiful, isn't it?
Your house is made of ice cream,
You look around and see,
Unicorns of all colours,
Your best friends and me,
We walk around together and see so many portals,
You see a black portal,
You peek through, but inside,
It has your darkest fear,
So I suggest we go to the Cloud Land portal,
You wonder what we will do there,
You follow me and then see a pod of clouds and candy,
You wish you could stay forever,
But you have to go now.

Lyra Shiels (9)
Braywood CE First School, Oakley Green

Amarah And The Chocolate Factory

C hocolate factories are my favourite
H appy people work hard
O dd chocolate at the factory
C hocolate cake I see
O range chocolate around me
L oads of fun
A n exciting place to visit
T hinking well and helping
E veryone is here

F riend is Douglas
A marah finds the golden ticket
C hocolate everywhere
T he ticket gleams with gold
O bjects are glamourous
R ich chocolate with caramel
Y ummy taste everywhere I go.

Amarah Teymorian (9)
Braywood CE First School, Oakley Green

Once Upon A Dream

There was a beautiful pink house with flowers and glitter all over the house
I met a unicorn who was called Violet
I met the unicorn in the forest
I felt so excited and happy
Then a young woman came and opened the door for me and Violet
She sat me down on a chair with a cup of tea in her hand
I felt so comfortable
After I had the cup of tea we all went outside
Then I saw a dancing dragon
Then the dragon roared and it started chasing me
I wanted it to stop
Then I woke up and found myself snug in my bed.

Orla Byrne (9)
Braywood CE First School, Oakley Green

A Lonely Ride

I woke up, feeling like it was a dream.
So it is!

I woke up lonely but in a glass mansion.
Then I realise I am a kid!
Though I can't get out, I feel energetic.
So I search every room and find a bedroom.

Then I ran downstairs and found a dog!
Not so lonely now!

I throw a ball to play with the dog
And then sleep with him.

Then, I woke up to my parents and a little apartment room.

Caden Cherry (8)
Braywood CE First School, Oakley Green

Mythical Creatures

I'm in a land I don't recognise,
Seeing giant gleaming eyes,
I take a step forward through the smoke,
Only to realise it's all a joke,
Just friendly creatures all around,
Some big, some small, some friendly sounds,
I'm glad it's not what I thought before,
Otherwise, I'd be on mission abort,
Suddenly, I wake up, I can't say bye,
I hope we can meet again sometime.

Noah Jones (8)
Braywood CE First School, Oakley Green

Willy Wonka's Chocolate Factory

Chocolate river, chocolate trees, sweets all around and candy bees
Oompa Loompas dancing to the slow tune
Edible things all around and candyfloss clouds floating past the macaroons.
I don't want to ever say goodbye to this wonderful sight
I wish I could stay here for my whole life.
Oompa Loompa Doopity Doo that's the end of my poem for you.

Lara-Jayne Kinane (8)
Braywood CE First School, Oakley Green

My Little Unicorn

I have a little unicorn,
It likes to dance and play.
I take it out for walks and feed it every day.

I have a little unicorn,
It sparkles and it shines.
It has big, beautiful wings
So that it can fly.

I have a unicorn,
The nicest I've ever met.
It is my opinion that it is the best pet.

Alys Lancaster (9)
Braywood CE First School, Oakley Green

Mystical Snow Land

I awake with the sight of snow,
Snowflakes drip on my nose,
My friends are there with me,
Shivering with glee,
This magical land, I do not get,
I am glad that we have met,
Fire crackles while snow falls,
My heart drifts away,
Like rivers flow.

Mia Komal (8)
Braywood CE First School, Oakley Green

Magical World Of Love

M y dream has come true,
A fairy always comes to me,
G listening sun sparkles,
I see unicorns with glee,
C rystals are bright and beautiful,
A lovely smell of roses,
L ight clouds cover the sky.

Kiran Uppal (9)
Braywood CE First School, Oakley Green

Pokémon

When I slump myself into bed
And rest my head
I close my eyes
And when I open them again
I see Pokémon left and right
I go on adventures, they're all by my side
And say, "Bye, see you again!"
And when I wake up I say to myself
It was awesome.

Humphrey Kinloch (8)
Braywood CE First School, Oakley Green

Happy World

I wake up,
The sun is shining,
I walk around,
I see a horse in front of me,
It's dancing,
Dragons surround me,
Fairies are shining,
Happy dreams come to me,
I never want to get out.

Sophia Mezzena Walker (9)
Braywood CE First School, Oakley Green

Drawing

D andelions floating
R oses red
A nimals galloping
W ater blue
I vy poisonous
N ature leaves
G rass green

My drawings can be seen.

Jasmine Smallwood (10)
Braywood CE First School, Oakley Green

Wales

W ater still
A nd daffodils sway near an eerie bay.
L ots of sheep and they go peep.
E xcitement booms in the rooms.
S o much fun with my mum.

Dylen Thomas-Dibb (9)
Braywood CE First School, Oakley Green

Dream World

Diya and Mia, lot of inspiration as dandelions,
Sway as the rumbling ocean plays,
Beneath the bay, where they play,
The clock ticks as my heart beats.

Diya Narang (8)
Braywood CE First School, Oakley Green

Lost In A Woodland

I found myself in the centre of a creepy, spooky woodland,
How I ended up here I don't understand,
As I stare around me I shiver,
Suddenly, I hear something coming from the river,
I hear an ear-piercing shriek,
I step forward and take a quick peek,
I glance left and right
But there is absolutely nothing in sight,
Eerie whispers are carried through the cold, dusty air,
I know something horrifying is there,
It must be some sort of ghost or spirit,
It went past me, I'm sure I felt it,
I forced my legs to carry on walking through the woods,
As I heard my name being called I pulled up my hood,
Rapidly, there was a flash of white,
The lightning gave me a fright,
The loud, flashing lightning growled,
All of the wolves howled,
A shadow appeared next to the tree,
Its face was pale and its eyes full of greed,

As it comes closer I'm filled with dread,
Sweating, I wake up to find I'm safe at home in bed.

Belkys Nsiri (11)
Calshot Primary School, Great Barr

Demons In A Nightmare

Go to sleep dear,
You don't have anything to fear,
Or do you?
Maybe not,
Or maybe so,
But now it's time for you to go.

So go to bed with your haunted head,
All these dreams are made up of illusions,
But hopefully, it doesn't cause you much confusion.
In the land of dreams,
Things are not always as they seem.
They may seem real,
But don't believe what you feel.

Fight the demons as you may,
They prey upon your distant days.
But as you sleep just remember,
These demons will fade and you will not surrender.

All this misconception,
Is the demons causing disruption.
Deep in your head,
When you are asleep in your bed.

With your thoughts on your own,
Causing your mind to be blown.
Out into space,
No, this isn't a race.
Put your life into perspective,
These demons are just infective.
They will go,
In about a minute or so.

Holly Stonehouse (11)
Calshot Primary School, Great Barr

Dear Diary, My Pink Dress

Dear Diary, wrote the girl,
I've got a new dress that puffs up when I swirl,
It's pink and sparkly, with sequins all over,
My mom said it's lucky, like a four-leaf clover,
My dad hates it, but I don't know why,
He said it's time to say goodbye,
People say it's flashy, some people say it's cool,
But my dad said I look like a big ol' fool.

My mom brought me some makeup as well on the side,
With a makeup book and everything, to use as a guide,
I put bronzer on my lips, blush on my eyes,
A lash brush hit my pupil and I nearly cried,
Makeup's not for me,
My pink dress is all I see,
It's my favourite item of clothing,
Like most people are assuming,
My very pink, sparkly dress,
Is better than all the rest,
She woke up and her head was full of delight,
But her lovely, pink dress was nowhere in sight.

Aaliyah Heaven (11)
Calshot Primary School, Great Barr

Twice Upon A Dream

In the depths of darkness, I wander alone.
A labyrinth of shadows, my heart made of stone.

The emptiness stretches far, a never-ending sea.
A void devours hope, something that fears me.

But then, a glimmer of light, a shimmer of gold.
A dream of a beach, where sunlight is always bold.

The sand is golden and there is a crystal sea,
A dream that fills my heart with glee.

The palm trees sway, the seagulls soar away
As I bask in the warmth of the sun-kissed day.

The water splashes at my feet, a soothing sound.
A lullaby that drowns out the emptiness around.

The beach is my Heaven, my safe place,
The place I feel calm, without any harm.
The peaceful paradise with an exotic charm.

Ishpinder Kaur (11)
Calshot Primary School, Great Barr

Childhood

One night I had a dream,
But not of the stars that shine and gleam,
Not of a monster under my bed,
Not of a pounding in my head,
I'll gnash and gnaw,
Until I'm raw,
Wish I could go back,
The brain that I lack,
But I can't stop ageing,
My youth is fading,
If I wake up now I'll shout and scream,
But it's ageing, it's going to be mean,
Life changes,
Turning pages,
Can't be young forever,
But can't handle the pressure,
Am I ageing,
Or am I trapped,
Is life about to unravel and unwrap,
In my arms?

Harps Skye (11)
Calshot Primary School, Great Barr

The Mirage

They call your name again and again
You feel like you're about to go insane
Finally, you have escaped that deadly place
Only to find out that it wasn't the end of the race
Work never ends
So you need to make amends.

You shudder at the thought of his face
And you quickly tie your shoelace
You sprint across the hall
Only to meet up with a wall.

The wall was anything but ordinary
It was extraordinary
It was filled with colour and light
And would make your face shine with delight.

Juwairiyah Kazi (10)
Calshot Primary School, Great Barr

Deceiving Dreams

While sleeping, I found a dream so brief,
A moment's joy, a flash of relief.
A beautiful meadow filled with flowers bright,
A gentle breeze through the night.
But then a twist did suddenly appear,
A turn of events so dark and clear.
A dream became a nightmare trip,
And all my joy began to rip.
In this dark dream, I felt such fear,
As figures crept and shadows were near.
Their laugh that echoed in my ear,
And as I woke up, I felt a tear.

Vimaljot Singh (9)
Calshot Primary School, Great Barr

My Dream

O ne day, I was in my bedroom with my sloths and mum.
N ext, I went back downstairs after I was playing with a
C at, because I was bored, so I went back to bed.
E very day, I have the same dream.

U ntil I had a different dream about a unicorn
P *lop*, the unicorn fell on the floor on her feet she loves
O ctopi because her friend was an octopus because
N o one like her has eight legs, so she thought it was cool.

A fter, I met a sloth called Sammy.

"**D** on't be naughty, Sammy," I said.
"**R** emember your nice manners," I said.
E lephants love Sammy, so they become friends,
A nd they love me too.
M aybe you can come, you're friends with everyone in the world.

Skyla Freestone (9)
Clenchwarton Community Primary School, Clenchwarton

Dancing Queen

I'm happiest when I dance, filled with joy,
The music takes me to a different place,
The bright lights of the studio excite me,
I just need a little more help,
As I step off the stage I see a familiar face,
Surely it's not her, how can that be?
It looks like her, the same black hair,
But why would Charli D'Amelio be here?
"I've come to help Esme,
I've heard she's so good,
Show me your moves girl,
Let's see what you've got,
I'll help you become the best you can be,
Let's get on the stage with the lights,
West End here we come,
Tomorrow the moon!"

Esme Turner (8)
Clenchwarton Community Primary School, Clenchwarton

Night Fright

I close my eyes and drift to sleep,
It's warm in bed, so comfy, so dark,
I hear a noise, what is that sound?
Is it thunder, or is it a growl?
I listen carefully, not daring to breathe,
I grab at Esme's arm for support,
She wakes with a jump, what's that?
We look at each other with fear in our eyes,
A paw reaches out from under the bed,
"It's okay girls, I'm friendly, my name's Fred,
Esme is still scared, so hides under the duvet,
"My name's Brookie, will you be my friend?"
Of course I will, we can have fun,
Let's plan the day together, make dens and run.

Martha Turner (8)
Clenchwarton Community Primary School, Clenchwarton

Me And My Friend

Me and my friend,
We play together,
We have a bond that stays forever,
In my dream last night,
We went to Disneyland, which had a lot of light,
When the light faded away,
We were in an expensive hotel, which is where we lay.

We went outside only to see,
Someone giving us a key,
We were the only ones actually there,
So we didn't have to share.

That meant we didn't have to wait in a queue,
Even for the rides that were new,
We had the best of times,
We even got to eat junk food like gummy slime.

Isabella Wells (9)
Clenchwarton Community Primary School, Clenchwarton

My Dreams

M y dreams are wonderful, as wonderful as they can be.
Y our dreams and my dreams are also very unique.

D aydream in the day and dream in the night.
R ight above your head, there is a starry sky.
E very day and every night, dream about something you want to come true.
A beautiful dream can be the best for you.
M ake dream time anytime you want.
S ometimes if you can't dream, just close your eyes and think of something you want to do.

Olivia Oczos (8)
Clenchwarton Community Primary School, Clenchwarton

Once Upon A Dream

The lights are bright
My chest is tight
I close my eyes
Block the noise
Of all the cheers and howling rain
With one big breath and steady myself
The next few moments feel like life or death
Eyes reopen. The silence is loud
Not a single noise from the crowd
My moment to shine
I shoot, I score
My teammates roar
While I celebrate, I fall to my knees
Victory is ours
Training for every minute on the pitch
Blood, sweat and tears
For years and years.

Daniel Dolby (9)
Clenchwarton Community Primary School, Clenchwarton

Rainforest

R ain falls down at the speed of light
A nimals of all different colours, shapes and sizes
I nsects scattered on the floor
N octurnal animals come alive at night
F ragrant plants fill the air
O rangutans play happily in the trees
R ubber trees create a colourful sight
E ndless green leaves dance in the wind
S nakes slither around the forest floor
T rees grow tall, reaching above the canopy.

Henry Neve (8)
Clenchwarton Community Primary School, Clenchwarton

The Goat

T he dream that I have each and every night, is to be a professional footballer,
H olding the champion's trophy high in the beautiful sky,
E ntering the pitch with my heart beating as fast as Mbappé dribbling the ball.

G oing from match to match with my teammates by my side,
O nly two minutes in and I've scored a goal,
A t Anfield Stadium, it's victory again,
T he crowd cheering my name, Noah!

Noah Ridge (8)
Clenchwarton Community Primary School, Clenchwarton

Dreaming

D reaming is a part of life,
R esting your eyes is a part of dreaming,
E ngland is a small country, but it has big dreams,
A iming high is what we need to do,
M aking dreams come true, if they don't we will work hard.

B ig dreams will come true if we work hard together as a team,
I nside of us somewhere is a little bit of happiness and love,
G reat dreams will come true somewhere in our lives!

Grace Burrell (9)
Clenchwarton Community Primary School, Clenchwarton

Imagination

I nteresting things here and there,
M agnificent stories in my head,
A mazing creatures come to life,
G listening stars above my head,
I magination can take you anywhere,
N ighttime adventures await,
A dream in every sleep,
T ravel through divergent dimensions,
I nto the unknown,
O pen up your mind,
N ever give in on your dreams.

Charlie Fisher (8)
Clenchwarton Community Primary School, Clenchwarton

My BFF Dream

M y bright sky,
Y ou and me together,

B e you and be me,
F riends dance and have fun,
F ollow yourself into a magical dream,

D ream to your destination and get higher,
R emind me, so I can think of my dream,
E very time I see my friend, I smile,
A sk a friend to be by your side,
M ia, be me.

Mia Meek (8)
Clenchwarton Community Primary School, Clenchwarton

Candyfloss

C harlotte's dream. I,
A m flying
N ot being alone in believing it
D reams are inspiring when you are together
Y ou can see pretty clouds like candyfloss
F lying in the air
L ying in the sky
O n top of the clouds, the rainbows shine
S miling about the dream
S aying goodbye to the dream once again.

Charlotte Chapman (8)
Clenchwarton Community Primary School, Clenchwarton

Bright Star

B ed is where I have my dreams
R ight above my head is the star
I can hear it speaking to me
G iving lots of positivity
H appy my star is telling me
T reat people kindly it says to me

S haring kindness from far away
T ake the star's advice
A nd we can learn
R espect for everyone.

Harper Comley (8)
Clenchwarton Community Primary School, Clenchwarton

Fairy Dream

F un with magical fairies,
A ir is around you like fairies are,
I s a dream the place you want to be,
R ight is the fairy way, left is the unicorn way,
I t's fun to be with magical things,
E ven when the stars are out at night fairies are too,
S o get comfy, fairies are coming your way.

Megan Burch (9)
Clenchwarton Community Primary School, Clenchwarton

Magical

M agical is you,
A fter all people can always be magical,
G reat people use it to help others,
I ndependent feelings are heard,
C asting magic takes practice to help,
A ccepting others and ourselves,
L asting magical people will change us forever.

Evie Buckingham (9)
Clenchwarton Community Primary School, Clenchwarton

Dream

D ifferent animals in this land are as happy as can be
R hinos with wings amongst other fabulous creatures I can see
E xtraordinary birds with tails flying above my head
A s tigers with dots eat pieces of bread
M y amazing dreams can take me anywhere.

Bella Godfrey (8)
Clenchwarton Community Primary School, Clenchwarton

Life And Dreams

Feel stuck in-between
Life and dreams
They seem to be mixed together
Leaving me unsure of what is real
What if it's all one big dream?
When am I going to wake up?

Alyssa Doy (8)
Clenchwarton Community Primary School, Clenchwarton

Snacks

What I like most in the world is snacks!
If you want to know more here are some hacks,
I open the cupboard and here I see,
A lovely box of crackers looking at me,
My mum says it is important to have five a day,
So I quickly eat my fruit and throw the leftovers away.
Now it's time for creamy cakes,
So Mum and I have to bake!
We weigh, sift and mix and then put it in the oven,
Then cakes we have, more than a dozen.
At school, I look for my snack,
I wondered what did she pack.
I eat my snack and down it goes,
Don't worry, not all the way to my toes!
My snack helps to feed my brain,
So that at school I do not wain,
So that's the message I want to send,
Snacks are the best and that's the end!

Abigail Green (7)
Gorseland Primary School, Martlesham Heath

Dare To Dream

Close your eyes and let your imagination fly away,
See pictures of where you wish to be one day.
Let the colours of when your heart takes command,
To paint the picture of your dream and place it in your hand.
Hold on tightly and it can go,
I saw a ballerina and danced with the flow.
I love my dreams but not nightmares,
Dreams are funny, dreams are nice, and dreams can also fight!
A daring adventure starts here, a dream is amazing.
Magic and fun,
In my dream, I went for a run.
I had a dream,
How I live is who I am,
Dreams are possible,
Dare to dream.

Hoorain Syed (8)
Gorseland Primary School, Martlesham Heath

Monster Dragon

M oving up and down, monster dragons go everywhere,
O rgans arrive at Monster Universe,
N owhere is the answer to where I will go,
S uperpowers start to come,
T he Growler Man arrives with
E vil SpongeBob SquarePants at his side,
R oblox Galaxy, come to me.

D ragon Land is the worst,
R obins are dark red,
A strange feeling eats into my mind,
G orgeous magic surrounds me,
O rgan music starts to play all around me,
N owhere to be seen,
S uperpowers arrive to me.

Benjamin Maximo Armengol (8)
Gorseland Primary School, Martlesham Heath

My Three Dreams

I dreamt that I played football,
And I played in front of a crowd,
I scored against the super strikers,
And the fans were really proud.

I dreamt that I was a princess
And that I saved the day,
From the disgusting bugs making a mess,
And yes, I scared them away.

I dreamt that I was a vet,
I gave the animals a cure,
I cared for a dog
Who was sick on the floor.

Brooke Holland (7)
Gorseland Primary School, Martlesham Heath

Monsters

M assive hairy faces staring at you
O minous footsteps wearing no shoes
N imble fingers pulling the duvet
S lithering shadows sneaking away
T eeth as sharp as a knife
E yes so wide there's nowhere you can hide
R umbling noises from behind the curtain
S urely it was a monster, I'm certain!

Jacob Alam (7)
Gorseland Primary School, Martlesham Heath

My Dream Holiday

In my dreams, on holiday,
I would go on a run in the sun
And it would be fun!

I would sit by the sea
Looking at a palm tree.
I would eat ice cream;
This is a wonderful dream.

I went into the pool to get cool.
Was it a dream, or...

Wait, was that ice cream?

Olivia Pitt (8)
Gorseland Primary School, Martlesham Heath

Endless Dreams

In endless dreams, a world so wide,
Where thoughts and wishes collide,
Slumber's realm where hope lives,
Into the journey that sleep gives,
We fall into many dreams,
Delightful and peaceful,
But nightmares often make us tearful.

Nightmares, they are the worst,
I sometimes think they want me to burst,
Or when in the movies when the monster would eat me first,
Not like I fall into the dream headfirst.

I see smoke coming out from over there.
Spiders crawling as they come out from nowhere!
I become nervous as they stare.
I can feel the temptation of death coming near…

I start running on the endless floor.
Hoping they will stop chasing me once and for all.
I start to run faster and faster as they are light no more.
Snakes slithering in the dark, in the distance, I see sparks.

I run out of breath and hope for the best.
I slowly close my eyes hoping I come to reality.
Finally, I wake up.
It's not the effect I normally feel
Oh well, I guess it's not such a big deal.

Fathmah Abid (11)
Hamilton College, Hamilton

Swift Dreamer

Dreams, it's something we all talk about
But can't seem to achieve, NYC Olympics 2030
That's my dream.

Running is my dream,
But I feel lost with nowhere to go,
The finish is ahead,
But competition strikes crossing the line,
Just in time all the hope is all gone.

I pick myself up and work hard,
Build stamina, determined and happy,
Training every day, to be the female Usain Bolt,
Be 25 in Forbes 30 under 30,
That's my dream.

2nd shot at 100m sprint, on your mark *go*, off I go
Still 2nd place but suddenly overtake the competitor.
All that hard work paid off! Gold medal,
Standing on the podium waving my country's flag.
Now that's my dream!

Bella Babalola (11)
Hamilton College, Hamilton

Spider

Scared while tiny.
Little horrifying spiders crawled up the tree.
I couldn't move my legs;
They were frozen.

Panting when a larger spider fell down
From a slim old tree.

Inside the tiny hut where I live,
Thousands and millions of terrifying spiders,
Long hairy legs and billions of eyes.

Then I see something in the distance.
Everything is happening too fast.

Deathly black spiders, bigger than the skyscrapers.
It had poison coming out of its mouth.

Every spider started to look at me with a death stare.
I see something in the distance; hope!
Suddenly, I can move!

Running to the place that I see,
But as I got near, I woke up.

Kavata Velle (11)
Hamilton College, Hamilton

The Kingdom

The grass, itchy, covering my face,
I get up and find I'm in a magical place,
Where the trees are yellow and the cities blue,
And there are cute little gnomes living in a shoe,
I look into the distance and spot something gold,
A palace of sorts, but all of a sudden I'm wearing a blindfold,
I wake up in my bed but then, going back to sleep, knowing this is a dream,
I can set it to any theme,
I take off the blindfold and get a shiver of cold,
As I realise that I'm in the Palace of Gold,
I gaze upon a throne a bit smaller than usual,
But just the right size for it to be beautiful,
I jump on a unicorn and burst through the palace,
I'm free and happy at last.

Ben Psaila (11)
Hamilton College, Hamilton

Controversial

C alm a quiet sea, singing its song,
O n the rock, the mermaids lie and they do no wrong.
N ot a cloud in sight, it is very, very bright.
T he unicorns fly high up in the sky.
R ain as soft as silk.
O ver the hill, where spiders stay.
V ery clever dragons live for that magical day.
E verybody is flying free, but not for long, you soon shall see.
R ain and thunderstorms, they'll never let us be!
S wamp monsters rise and angels fall.
I n the village, a scream comes from all.
A massive monster emerges from the pond.
L and and sea, they have all gone.

Caleb Browning (11)
Hamilton College, Hamilton

My Nightmare

I ran and ran through forests of pine,
It was dark, chills running down my spine,
I stopped to breathe, one... two... three...
But a sinister voice was right behind me.
I turned and looked, there stood a clown.
A fright, a jumpscare, I was knocked down.
Trapped in a cage, a scary clown in my face,
I gave a shout, but he could not be erased.
Letting snakes out, I thought death was near
Cobras, boas, pythons... the height of my fear.
As they were about to bite, I woke with a start.
My cousin shouted, "Circus tickets," which warmed my heart.

Misha Shafiq (11)
Hamilton College, Hamilton

Blue Birds

Blue birds flying over my head
Gliding in the afternoon sky
The bird's wings fluttering through the air
Air on the bird's heads lifted in the breeze
Getting their nest ready for the spring ahead
High up, the birds are gathering leaves
The last of the cold breeze blasts through the branches
New warmer breezes are coming
The birds are ready for a long adventure in the blue sky
To wake up from the long winter to slumber with sunshine in their eyes
The birds are now ready for a new season and adventures.

Blair Kinnoch (11)
Hamilton College, Hamilton

In My Dreams

In my dreams, I wake with a fright,
It looks like I'm going to fly tonight.
Slowly I creep out of bed,
Crazy thoughts fill my head.
I stand on the balcony ledge and feel the breeze.
Suddenly my mind is at ease.

I put one foot out,
Then the other.
I'm standing on thin air,
Wind blowing in my hair.

I love the balcony, flying high,
Taking off into the sky.
I fly and fly,
Waving bye to my deserted bed,
In my dreams.

Shannon Olusola-Johnson (11)
Hamilton College, Hamilton

Our Beautiful Game

On the green field where dreams take flight,
Players unite, with all their might.
With every pass and every goal,
Football's magic begins to unfold.
The roar of the crowd, the thunderous cheer,
As heroes emerge, their victory is near.
A dance of skill. A game of grace,
Football's beauty in every chase.

From grassroots to stadiums, the love remains,
A universal language that forever sustains.
In the game, we find joy, passion and pride,
Football is a timeless thrill that never subsides.

Blaine Robson (11)
Hamilton College, Hamilton

The Driving Clown

The clown driving through the town.
His car is a dark brown.
As I look at his frown
It makes me drown in dread.
I run faster than Usain Bolt.
And if I made one fault, I will be in my grave.
As I run around the corner, I get a big fright as I see a big light.
Running back around the corner and into my house.
In my house, I see a mouse with big teeth which fills me with more dread.
Then I realise I'm safe at home in bed!

Rafe Chesworth (11)
Hamilton College, Hamilton

Nightmare

N ot Again! I scream, "I hate this dream!"
I t lingers in my head once I'm awake,
G iggles that sound sinister,
H orrific screeches, "Ahh!"
T errifying monsters that tower over me,
M aybe they are friendly? I warily implore,
A re you? I calmly ask.
R oar! It bellows.
E verything is okay, I wake up and sigh, "It was just a dream."

Rebecca Coughlan (11)
Hamilton College, Hamilton

The Abandoned Town

I went to sleep with a frown
Woke up later in an abandoned town
I shot up and then back down
Why did I have to be in a dream with a clown?
I would have rather been in one where I wielded a crown
Or one with a cyber town so overgrown
Or one with a special dog with a magic bone
Well, back to the clown; it spoke to me in a dead-low tone
The clown jumped at me as I awoke on my own.

Harris Cunningham Mason (11)
Hamilton College, Hamilton

Untitled

D affodils brighten up the sky with their bright yellow glow,
R oaring dinosaurs roaming around giving people rides,
E veryone playing in a land of sweets,
A never-ending jawbreaker that will make your jaw ache,
M assive milkshakes that are bigger than the sea,
S kies filled with cotton candy clouds.

Kathleen Bullen (11)
Hamilton College, Hamilton

Unicorn

U nder the stars, I saw a unicorn fly by.
N ever trust what you see in your dreams.
I t may be an evil flying unicorn,
C hasing innocent people,
O ver to its evil lair.
R ed horns on its head like a devil,
N ever mess with this fiend.

Tafara Mutezo (11)
Hamilton College, Hamilton

Dreams

D arkest hour into the night,
R ealising I was in a dream with fright.
E very time I close my eyes tight,
A spooky clown is ready to fight.
M onsters dance in the dim light,
S lowly, I drift off into the night.

Ethan Akun (11)
Hamilton College, Hamilton

A Space Adventure

A s I drift into another world, playing with my friends, I close my eyes and open them only to see a

S pace background. I blink and blink again. No! It can't be! Swirling colours of
P urple, dark blue, hot pink and black decorate a starry sky
A mazed but confused, I float around
C uriously looking for my friends
E ventually, I realise they are not there

A nd I look around to explore, when I bump into a unicorn, the same
D ark colours like the ones around me
V eronica is her name. She shows me around and at the
E nd of the journey, she took me to a planet
N o End To Fun it was called. Over there, I saw
T oys and toys galore. I bought a bubble wand and an
U nderwater-patterned portal appears. I go th-
R ough but it turns out it's an
E nd to the journey.

Unaysa Zakir (9)
Oak Tree Primary School, Mitcham

Peace Has Finally Come

As I fall asleep, into a dream
My brother is downstairs watching a meme.
Peace started covering my life,
Everyone will stop using knives.
The war has finally stopped,
Now the floor can finally be mopped.
Me and Yasmin go to clean the street,
Where Palestine and Israel come to meet.
Wow, we have got a lot of cleaning to do,
We need to do Israel too.
Wow, we made Palestine and Israel sparkle,
What? ... Who's Markle?
All our hearts have been mended,
There are people sitting at home, wow I feel offended.
I feel so tired,
I wasn't even hired.
Saarah wake up, wake up
I did all the hard work and I got a face of water in a cup.
It was all just a dream,
And my brother is still watching memes.

Saarah Zahid (11)
Oak Tree Primary School, Mitcham

Arsenal Is The Best!

Arsenal is the best,
Smashing Man City,
It's such a pity,
That they lost,

Stepping on a vast field,
My heart's in my throat,
In the audience I think I heard a goat,
I'm going crazy,

I'm getting lazy,
Martinelli's winging,
Man City's goal hanging,
Running up and down the Etihad Stadium,

Fouls, whistles, boos and shouts,
Both teams are scoring,
This match is getting boring,
The score is three to one,

This match is nearly done,
I don't think this is fun,
The ball hits the net,
The final whistle blows,

We've defeated our goal,
Arsenal is the best,
Then the alarm goes,
It's my mum waking me from my rest!

Yusuf Usman (10)
Oak Tree Primary School, Mitcham

Nightmare

I look left, I look right, where could I be?
In a Monster Land with a key!
To unlock a chamber of secrets,
As I stare deeply at Cerberus.
Deep thoughts rumbling in my mind,
Will I ever find it?

I found a girl called Tasnim;
She's a dream!
I shine like a beam,
I'm very keen.
I also see a very good crime scene,
Suddenly I woke up to find,
I'm safe at home
With my family behind.

Aisha Shahzad (10)
Oak Tree Primary School, Mitcham

Under The Sea

S wimming
T urtles
A lgae
R ainbow starfishes
F ishes
I cy cold water
S eahorses
H aving fun

O ctopus
C oral
E xtremely big wave
A mazingly clear ocean
N atural sea creatures

M agical mermaids
E xtremely cold ocean
R acing to the sea
M ega sandcastle
A mazing mermaids
I gloo made of sand
D ogs playing.

Elodie (7)
Perranporth Community Primary School, Liskey Hill

Doctor Who, Nabitt And Rabbit And Rex Fury

Doctor Who,
Heroic as can be,
With a blue and red suit like Superman,
And is really strong,
He kicks!
He flies!
He fights for the right!
Who is this strong, heroic man?

Nabbit,
Mean as can be,
Always lurking in people's houses while they're asleep,
Snap,
Rap,
Crack,
Who is this monster?

Rabbit,
Mean as can be,
Making crime in town all day long,
Stealing money,
Snap,

Crack,
Yap,
Who is this heroic mean person?

Rex Fury,
Mean as can be,
Making crime all day long,
Having workouts,
Snap,
Yap,
Crack,
Who is this crime monster?

Ezra Law (7)
Perranporth Community Primary School, Liskey Hill

Evylin And Topaz

E nchanted forest!
V ery sparkly!
Y ay! I'm a fairy!
L ollipops are the best!
I ce castle!
N ately!

A nd there's a festival!
N ately, the sun fairy!
D ungeons are dangerous!

T opaz is cute!
O ctopus lives nearby!
P olly the party fairy!
A n owl!
Z ooming by!

Freyja Ballinger (7)
Perranporth Community Primary School, Liskey Hill

Footballer Dreams

The footballer is athletic, swift and strong,
The footballer dribbling, passing and saving,
The footballer is magnificent!

The footballer is fit, healthy and quick,
The footballer, tackling, fouling, hurting,
Will the footballer play again?

The footballer, brilliant, injured, famous,
The footballer, passing, saving, dribbling,
The footballer is back to top form.

Danny Williams (7)
Perranporth Community Primary School, Liskey Hill

Monster Dreams

M ergals live in the castle
O gres live in caves and grow flowers and vegetables
N osub is a sea monster
S teel monsters, shiny and mistaken for steel
T rags are yellow and eat vegetables
E ast monsters always travel east!
R ags live in your carpet and eat carpet!
S tonks are very stinky and are found hiding in a bin.

Elsie Smith (7)
Perranporth Community Primary School, Liskey Hill

The Wizard School

Wizard School
Like a lonely weird bird
Flying every morning in circles
Will I ever go?

Kings Cross, there, in a secret place
If you are nervous, run
Bravely run into the wall
The time it closes is 12 o'clock.

Wizard School pictures float in the sky
A Nimbus 2000 broom
A spotty, stripy, blue castle
A very dangerous place.

Maya O'Brien (7)
Perranporth Community Primary School, Liskey Hill

The Lonely Clown

A clown lived in a carnival,
Shut down, lonely and afraid,
The clown, adventure, enchanted forest, monster!
The clown saw a sparkly, white unicorn save him!
They kept going,
They saw a fairy,
It gave him wings!
The clown was bad,
He invited his dragon spider!
The creature attacked them,
Muhahahaha!

Emily Carter (7)
Perranporth Community Primary School, Liskey Hill

Surf And Skate

S urf,
U se your surfboard,
R un to the sea,
F un in the sea.

A ginormous wave!
N ot a gnarly wave,
D angerous waves!

S kate,
K ick, flip,
A n amazing trick!
T op of the ramp,
E xtremely dangerous drop in!

Noah Kershaw (7)
Perranporth Community Primary School, Liskey Hill

Hello Kitty And Friends

Hello Kitty is eating lots of cupcakes
Eating in the sparkly water
Badtz-Maru coming to save the village
He slashes his sword
She is still gobbling cake
The sword misses
Hello Kitty is back to normal
The village is saved
They ate cupcakes
Time to party.

Pixie Griffiths Grant (8)
Perranporth Community Primary School, Liskey Hill

Dreams

Castle misty in the distance,
Like a grey hot air balloon,
Flying, floating, fluttering,
Will we get inside at all?

Closer, closer the horrifying gates open,
What lies behind no one knows,
Floating, fluttering, flying,
Why are we still alone?

Rory Lane (7)
Perranporth Community Primary School, Liskey Hill

The Candy Dream

Smartie king, crunchy, yummy delicious,
Like a chocolatey dream.

Eating, munching, digesting,
Will I ever get enough?

M&M queen, delightful, lovely, nice,
Like a sweetie dream,
Crunching, tasting, loving,
How many can I eat?

Amy Thomas (8)
Perranporth Community Primary School, Liskey Hill

The Marshmallow World

M agical and misty
A mazing and pink
R are
S oft and squidgy
H appy it makes
M e
A wesome
L umpy
L ong and luscious
O ften I eat them all
W arm in my belly.

Teddy Whiting (7)
Perranporth Community Primary School, Liskey Hill

Axolotls

Axolotls swimming,
In the bluey-green sea,
Wow, look how cute they are,
It's impossible-

Well, I think it is,
Probably is,
Hopefully I'm right,
Wow!

A turtle,
How cute,
Cute, cute, cute!

Maisie Palmer (7)
Perranporth Community Primary School, Liskey Hill

Sunny Beach

A cave, glimmering, glancing cave...
Went inside,
Caved in, scared, horrified!
Where are my parents?
Running, to break
Out of the darkness.
Shiny, see-through coral reef,
Axolotl, sea turtles too,
We're free.

Kirk Pietrasz (7)
Perranporth Community Primary School, Liskey Hill

Unicorns, Fairies And Me

Unicorn, purple, pretty, magical,
Like a butterfly,
Fluttering, flying, flickering,
How much magic do you have?
Fairies, wonderous, dreamy, cursed,
Like a pretty bird,
Dancing, laughing, harmless,
How far can you fly?

Bonnie Ansell (8)
Perranporth Community Primary School, Liskey Hill

Spider-Man Vs Green Goblin

Spider-Man never reveals himself,
Especially to his mother,
Except to Green Goblin,
His arch-nemesis!

Spider-Man always fighting crime
From Green Goblin,
Green Goblin has friends,
A lot of friends!

Lucas Chegwidden (7)
Perranporth Community Primary School, Liskey Hill

Dreams

F ootball,
O utside,
O ut of the stadium,
T aron my friend, was cold,
B ut a bat was around,
A scary man comes,
L et it come,
L et it, no, no!

Taron Aldridge (7)
Perranporth Community Primary School, Liskey Hill

Bubbles

B ubbles in the bath,
U se bubbles in the bath
B ubbles glide,
B ubbles flow,
L ights flowing in them,
E xtremely giant bubbles,
S oft bubbles.

Isaac Thomas (8)
Perranporth Community Primary School, Liskey Hill

The Wonder Garden Dream

There is a garden,
But not any garden, the Wonder Garden,
Pixies that are fluttery,
Pixies that are pretty,
Fairies who are beautiful,
Fairies that are sparkling.

Indie Hurley (7)
Perranporth Community Primary School, Liskey Hill

The Famous Footballer

F un
O ffside
O ld footballer
T eam Perranporth
B all
A ston Villa
L egendary footballer
L eague.

Harry Webber (7)
Perranporth Community Primary School, Liskey Hill

Untitled

Inside the cave,
I turned around,
Frowned,
Could I escape?
Being chased, got outside,

I didn't know where to go.

Harmony Grant (7)
Perranporth Community Primary School, Liskey Hill

The Gut-Eating Clown

The gut-eating clown, dark forest
With cries of despair,
From what's left,
From the things trying to destroy the clown.

Levi Schick (7)
Perranporth Community Primary School, Liskey Hill

Wonderland

As I swing down vines,
As I climb up trees,
As I feel the cool air and summer breeze,
As I go boating in a pond,
As I eat my favourite snacks,
As I cuddle my Chihuahuas, Nacho and Max.

When daffodils and dewdrops and bluebells bloom,
As I lie down and sing my songs in my treehouse room.

As I nibble on popcorn and watch Pegasus glide,
With my very best friends by my side.

As I stitch up my satchel,
As I clean up my mittens,
As I make up stories,
As I wander and play with baby kittens.

As I daydream,
As I cuddle in nooks,
As I code animations,

As I read my best books,
As I fly and soar, as I whoop and I laugh,
As I smile, as I fall, as I make a sturdy raft.

As I clamber and sprint and tiptoe and roll,
As I make cool glasses for me and that mole.

As I dance in the rain,
As I sing in the shower,
As I gasp when I find my cat has the power.

As I chase butterflies, as I drift and dream,
As I catch a ray of sunlight beam.

As I explore new forests, free to roam,
I'm actually tucked in bed, safe at home.

Amelie Callaway (10)
St Lawrence CE Primary School, Chobham

Squiggles And Me

Squiggles is my pet hamster,
She could be mistaken for a mole,
Her fur is silky soft
And she has teeny tiny milky white toes,
She has a little pink nose that reminds me of a mole,
She likes to make big hills
And cause quite a mess.

She covers her food and fills her water bowl
While busy rearranging her home.
Sawdust flies everywhere
Even covering her from head to toe
But she doesn't care
She's happy building her little home

My hamster is silly,
But my hamster is the best,
She likes to whiz around her exercise wheel,
Spinning around and around,
She makes me dizzy.
She likes to climb the sides of her cage,
And tries to chew through the bars,
Thinking how to plan her escape,
Little does she know I have my eye on her.

I love my hamster, she is the best,
She likes to dig and burrow,
Just like a mole.
I love the way she stuffs her cheeks,
With all her little treats.
My hamster is silly,
She reminds me of a mole,
She causes quite a mess,
But I wouldn't change her,
She's simply the best.

Skyla Bullock (7)
St Lawrence CE Primary School, Chobham

We Choose Positive Thoughts

Positive thoughts create hopeful feelings
And attract positive life experiences.
A positive mind looks for ways a task can be done,
A negative mind looks for ways it can't be done.
Being positive doesn't mean that everything is good
It's changing your mindset to see the good in everything.

Put your positive hats on,
Train your mind to see the good in everything.
Positivity is a choice.
The happiness of your positive thoughts depends on your life.
When you focus on the good, the good increases.
A great day that starts with a positive thought invites encouraging events throughout the day.
Cultivating positive thinking is not about the best,
It's about being the best you can be.

Jessica Cassini (9)
St Lawrence CE Primary School, Chobham

The Legend Dream!

The dragon's scales shimmer in the mist,
As I dream I also wish,
Oh, but hunters come to see the treasure that lies beneath,
Dragons live in the deep woods,
Darkness but there's a light that is misunderstood,
The unicorn colour of neon glimmers so brightly,
Protectors of forest both day and night,
Why seek it all over the fall,
Fly over rainbows, the colour of all,
Phoenix as red as a ruby light,
As soft as a feather,
As sweet as wildlife,
Troll the colour of vomit green,
As ugly as Venom,
And oh so mean!
As giant and destructive as dynamite!
Pirates as greedy as a pig in flight,
Vikings as violent as Ares the God of War!
The creatures of myth!
One and all!

Emily Igoe (7)
St Lawrence CE Primary School, Chobham

The Magic Key

Everyone has a dream,
But in mine, it's different from how it seems,
There are bicycles with three wheels,
Enormous pearls,
And twenty-four seals,
Ballerinas eating Twirls and Lego
Flowers in the ground,
Cold is hot and hot is cold,
Giants with no sound,
Hills that, most of the time, I roll on,
And bunnies with adorable noses,
SpongeBob catching jellyfish,
Bananas as tall as me from top to toe,
An amazing dish,
A treehouse full of books and games,
And my friends beside me,
One dog, fully trained,
Then I open the door,
With the magic key,
Now I wake up,
Ready for tea.

Alexa Cooke (10)
St Lawrence CE Primary School, Chobham

The Unicorn!

Unicorns, these funny things,
My sister likes them and they also have wings.
Design your own, do what you like,
Just don't let them give your friends a horrible fright.
Big, fat butterflies flying in the sky,
Morning rainbows and shifting skies.
Unicorns can be especially fat,
Doing cartwheels and all that.
Some like pooing cupcakes,
Some like hugging rainbows,
Some like playing with flamingoes!
Moustache penguins and marshmallow caverns, where lolly-lickers lurk
And fluffy pancakes beckon.
Unicorns can do many things,
As long as they're not horrifying.

Eve Lynch (9)
St Lawrence CE Primary School, Chobham

Getting Lost

G o and get scared, run, wild and anxious,
E xcept that you are lost, but stay precious!
T hrilling people are mean and heartless,
T ry and stay hugely harmless,
I nto the big, frightening darkness,
N egative wind gusts around in darkness,
G et all the understanding around the world, don't be careless.

L ots of people, be careful! Don't be careless,
O f all the world is dangerous. Don't be careless,
S tay safe in the world,
T hank you and that is all I have to say! Don't get cold!

Sadie Field (11)
St Lawrence CE Primary School, Chobham

My Pigeon's Life

Life as a pigeon is very tough.
Snipe, robin, tit and ruff,
City, wood, stream, tree,
High in the sky, as free as can be.

Falcon, hawk, kestrel, hobby,
On the lookout to catch a pidgey.
Feed on some seeds, no time to read.

Not like a woodpecker,
The pochard or the heron.
Small and quick, smooth and slick.

Grey storm out the blue,
Always trying to steal my food.
Lay an egg, let it wobble,
Unlike the turkey, *gobble, gobble, gobble.*

A pigeon's life is very tough,
Snipe, robin, tit and ruff.

Jack Arnitt (10)
St Lawrence CE Primary School, Chobham

Dragons

One lives in the sky, way up high.
One lives down below, where no one dares to go.
One dreams in mazes.
Another walks in the heavens.
One flies past glaciers.
One likes disguises.
One is a shimmering blue, sitting on a balloon.
One is a ruby-red, hiding in a shed.
One is a moulty catastrophe!
One is purple.
One is yellow.
One is spotty, dotty white.
One is green and zigzaggy.
One is wavy and slight.
Magical dragons flying around.
I hope you see one, too.

Darcy Toropov (8)
St Lawrence CE Primary School, Chobham

Dancer

Dancing around, a Swan Lake scene,
Toes tipped up, feathers prancing,
She's as beautiful as she has ever been,
Amazing as her arms wave around.
Oh! Such amazing dancing,
Moving around, she makes no sound,
Our swan, a beauty never to be found.
Prancing, oh, dancing.

She goes up, she goes down,
She goes left, she goes right.
She spins round and round,
As she shines all around.
Oh! What a look that she can share,
What a look for everywhere.

Abigail Draper (10)
St Lawrence CE Primary School, Chobham

Dancing In A Trance

Under the rain we dance
Singing and growing in a trance
Let the happiness flow within
Feel the music! Have some gin!

With the party now in fifth gear,
Laughter is all that you hear,
Within some dancing body-to-body,
You'll catch them being a little naughty,

Without a care in the world we dance,
Dancing as if it were our last chance,
'Til the rain stops and the sun rises,
Keep watching 'cause we're full of surprises!

Sinead Loveridge (9)
St Lawrence CE Primary School, Chobham

Dream The Impossible

I dream the impossible dreams,
Battling dragons, trolls, evil wizards,
And everything inbetween.

I have seen dazzling elephants, wolves,
And leopards fly by.
I'm not afraid to aim high,
Reaching for the sky.

My dreams have magic,
And I wish on shimmering stars,
I sometimes search for aliens on Mars.

Every day, I share my dreams with friends,
Because after all, love and friendship
Never ends!

Emelia Stacey (8)
St Lawrence CE Primary School, Chobham

Pandas!

I love pandas; they're snuggly and cuddly.
So come on, pandas, all around!

I love pandas; it could be red,
And of course, do roly pollies!

I love pandas!
There's red, brown, and black.
So come on, pandas, all around!

I love pandas,
They're so cute.
I wish I was one!

So come on, pandas, pandas everywhere!
So come on, pandas, all around!

Freddie Hunt (9)
St Lawrence CE Primary School, Chobham

My Dreams Are...

A pack of swimming seals,
And monkeys with banana peels.
Paper in a tear,
And donkeys climbing stairs.
Aliens playing football,
And me standing on a stall.
The tip of a hill,
And cupcakes paying a bill.
Humans with gills,
And cupcakes still paying the bills.
The sound of breaking glass,
And finally swaying grass.
Those are my dreams.

Nathan Cooke (9)
St Lawrence CE Primary School, Chobham

Cats

Cats, cats, all around me,
Further than the human eye can see.
Cats over here, cats over there,
Colours spreading everywhere.
Grooming, licking,
Sometimes kicking.
Sweet and cute,
A whole tribute.
Purring, growling,
Hissing, meowing.
Fluffy old pussy,
You are my toffee.
Ah! That's what they like,
Oh! What a wonderful sight.

Marygrace De Cillis (9)
St Lawrence CE Primary School, Chobham

Hawk

The hawk flies high overhead
As a small mouse tucks into bed
The hawk spies the mouse's tail
So it swoops down, only to fail
It soars back to the safety of the sky
Not realising the end is nigh
A cloud whisps, blocking its view
But you awaken, yes you
Slowly you rise out from your bed
Confused by what your mind just said.

Rafe Newton (10)
St Lawrence CE Primary School, Chobham

Dragons

D angerous, evil beast of the land,
R oars over the mountainous terrain,
A range of green, red, orange and blue shapes of beasts,
G reat, mighty, fire-based,
O n the map head East to West to find the best,
N orth and South, open your mouth,
S uper beasts, find them there.

Clarke Phelps (10)
St Lawrence CE Primary School, Chobham

Dreams, Dreams

Dreams, dreams
You have them all night
Frightening or calm
You still have a good night
Dreams of rainbows
Dreams of the dark
You always wake up
In a fright or in the light.

Harper Hobson (8)
St Lawrence CE Primary School, Chobham

Be Courageous

If you are courageous in all that you do,
Then your heart will be too.
Courage is the key to all you love and see,
It is in each and every one of us,
You just have to believe.

Cora Wilks (9)
St Lawrence CE Primary School, Chobham

Tiger

T errifying tiger on the prowl,
I n the emerald jungle,
G rowling at busy birds,
E agerly stalking its prey,
R oaring ferociously!

Poppy Brown (7)
St Lawrence CE Primary School, Chobham

Once Upon A Dream

Once upon a dream,
A boy ate strawberries and cream.
He fell into a hole,
And found a mole eating a troll.
The boy named the mole Dirty Cole.
Just remember, moles eat trolls.

Olivia Hunter (9)
St Lawrence CE Primary School, Chobham

Fire Fox

Fire fox explode it might
Flaming eyes shining bright
Fire fox beaming tail
Fire fox hear it wail.

Odessa Newton (7)
St Lawrence CE Primary School, Chobham

The Three Wonderful Wacky Lands

There were three magical, mystical, mysterious lands.
They all had something wacky and weird about them.
The first land was as jumpy and fun as jumping jellyfish.
Everybody wanted to visit this land.
You could see butterflies fluttering in the breezy wind and bunnies could be seen happily hopping in the distance.

The second land was nothing like the first.
Terrible storms would often occur
Everything was dull
Nothing was fun, no matter how much you tried
No matter the joke, it wouldn't be funny
I recommend with all my might, do not visit this boring land.

Oh this land is frightening
Creepy crawling spiders would crawl up your legs
Dark skies could be seen up above, including bats
Although because the sky was so dark and gloomy
They were hard to see.

Demons, monsters, ghouls and creepy clowns
They ruled this land and they didn't like visitors
Enter if you dare
They would greet you with a fright!

Eden Storrie (11)
St Mary's Primary School, Bathgate

Winterland

I touch the handle and heat swarms through me.
Instantly, I hear the drop of the key.
Then I'm in my dreams, travelling oh so far,
And I'm not even travelling by car.

I'm in my wonderful winter wonderland
And it makes me smile!
I feel like I could run for a mile!
I smell mince pies and it widens my eyes.

I run and run till I feel like I'm done.
Soft, crispy snow, covers the Earth's atmosphere.
I watch with grief as the snow disappears.
It falls off the branches and tickles my neck.

It isn't much, just a little speck.
My hands feel like cubes of ice
And that feeling isn't very nice.

I get funny butterflies in my tummy
And I begin to feel like I want my mummy!
I suddenly feel like a moody old Grinch,
So I decided to give myself a soft little pinch.

Boom! Bang!
And then I'm back
In the safe sound place I call,
Home sweet home!

Amelia Christie (10)
St Mary's Primary School, Bathgate

The Scary Dream

It was a normal Friday night
Holly was left home alone
The room was as dark as the sparkly night sky.

She was as scared as a lost boy.

She was about to turn on the TV
When she heard a *boom*, *bang* and *whoosh*!
Someone was in the house!

She ran up to her room
She locked the door
The room was dark and gloomy.

She heard footsteps coming up the stairs
She had no choice
She got her stuff ready
Someone opened the door
Holly jumped out the window.

But she doesn't make a landing. She flies up, up high.

She felt the clouds
They were as fluffy as a big, cosy teddy bear
Suddenly she falls on the rock-solid ground
Then she wakes up.

"Oh no, that was a scary dream," said Holly, running down the stairs.

Lilia Kay (10)
St Mary's Primary School, Bathgate

Spooky Dream

As the cat chases the rat,
Down the hallway, it was as dark as a scary mat,
It meowed and squeaked until I turned the light on,
It was as bright as bleach.

There was a rumble, then a crumble
Then *pow*! *Bang*!
Then the light started flickering like a star twinkling under the dark midnight sun.

As I quietly picked up the cat her warm fur
Was as warm as a crackling fire
Under the glistening summer sky.

She was soft and round, as sweet as an iced bun.
As I looked at the cat I knew we were going to have so much fun.

The cat looked at me with big green eyes and
I looked at her in amazement
As she began to double in size!

Gracie Shaw (10)
St Mary's Primary School, Bathgate

Volcanoes

On a sunny day, everyone was happy until...
Volcanoes wanted to erupt in the village!
Everyone screamed in panic,
Like a crowd of primary school kids shouting!

"What are we going to do?" someone shouted.
Two 9-year-olds saw a fire-breathing dragon!
Everyone was informed to hide from the dragon.

All of a sudden, the dragon died of the shiny, bright light.
"That's definitely wonderful winter weather!" said an old granny.
"Snow!" said all of the kids.
"Oh dear... " said some of the parents.
"Boom!" a little kid said, with their toy.

Kristiana Ramule (11)
St Mary's Primary School, Bathgate

Once Upon A Dream

Once upon a dream,
I was in Cat Land.
It was my cat, Storm and I who came here.

There are mountains of cats everywhere.
Even some drinking from chocolate fountains.
But as I look around,
Storm is nowhere to be found.

I look up and down
But I can't find him anywhere.
Suddenly, the Cat King named Feisty Fred
Jumps on my head and scratches it all over.

So I grab his tail and he begins to wail,
So I throw him into Dog Land.
Then I see Storm wrapped up
All warm so I pick him up.

And then I wake up
And Storm is sleeping beside me.

Emily Marshall (10)
St Mary's Primary School, Bathgate

Once Upon A Dream

Crashing and banging
I fell into Tayland
I woke up on The Eras Tour
I could hear Taylor singing songs
I was so excited, it was like meeting the king
After the show, I ended up in a millionaire's mansion
I looked around and saw a cat called Meridith meowing
I went upstairs and saw Taylor there
Singing her new songs
Bang! Crash!
The drums went
Her golden blonde hair shone like diamonds
As she gave me a big hug
Travis Kelce played on the TV
But everything comes to an end
It was time to go.

Erin Lumsden (11)
St Mary's Primary School, Bathgate

The Wavy Land

Nothing has prepared me for this strange land
All I could see was wavy birds
And wavy clouds twirling high above me.
I take a step forward
As nervous as can be
Stepping left and right, all I see
Is wavy things huddling around me.
Boom!
Something falls from the sky
It's wavy around
Me and my sister realise it's Wavy Land!
Suddenly wavy birds and wavy objects
Are surrounding me
Then I woke up in my room safe and sound.

Haniya Shahzad (10)
St Mary's Primary School, Bathgate

Once Upon A Dream

Splash Island in Spain,
Water canons filled with water,
Children having fun,
Fizzy Fanta,
Smash mash,
Ice barrels flying through the air,
The speed of light,
Splash slides go super speed,
The canons were rockets,
The frozen tree danced,
Underwater were orcas,
Going on a rampage,
Eating slimy fish,
The orcas jumped as high as a high jumper,
The children stepped gently into the puddle,
Splash.

James Greig
St Mary's Primary School, Bathgate

Once Upon A Dream

Once upon a time in Mashed Potato Land
It was the mashed potato parade
The sun blazed with anger
The sky as blue as the sea
Children laughing, children playing
Oh what a sound
You can smell cooking kitchens
And taste delicious snacks
Then go back home to go to bed
In the morning we'll have fun.

Ethan McGinty (11)
St Mary's Primary School, Bathgate

Once Upon A Dream

Once upon a dream,
There were pom-pom trees as soft as a cloud,
And beds made out of popsicle sticks.
The sky is made of paint,
And the ground is all made of oil pastels.
Children's laughter fills the air,
Babies grabbing their mother's hair,
And crying in their pram.

Roma Purdie
St Mary's Primary School, Bathgate

Dream, Dream, Dream

As the clock turned to nine o'clock, I went to bed.
Suddenly, I drifted off to sleep, then I started to dream.
I dreamt about being one of the best football players,
But I had to explore Dream Land.

It was flipped.

The trees were hanging upside down, like a bat,
Water races down like a race car.
White fluffy clouds beneath my feet.
I always dreamed of playing in the famous Anfield Stadium.

Ronan Carragher (7)
St Michael's Primary School, Newry

I Got Rid Of My Fright

One starry night I spotted a light
I went downstairs and I got a fright
The doorbell rang, I got another fright
I want to answer the door but it might be bright
I went upstairs to my room
I looked out of the window
No one was there
So I turned on the lights
To get rid of the fright
My mum and dad woke me up
And they said to me goodnight.

Mia Casey (8)
St Michael's Primary School, Newry

Fairy Meadow

One magical day in Fairy Meadow
The fields were as peaceful as flowers
Joy was there
There was blue air
The fairy queen was as proud as a sparkling light
Riding peaceful unicorns
Laughing like a warm sun
Leaves gliding like they're having good fun
Dreams filling the air
We are a wonderful pair.

Neasa Carragher (8)
St Michael's Primary School, Newry

Me Being A New Me

As I lie in bed,
Dreams fill my head,
I thought of myself swimming,
In water as blue as the sky.

My arms *swish, swash, swish,*
Sea creatures cheer me on,
My heart fills with joy,
I am finally a new me, like a butterfly,
But when I woke up I realised I was dreaming.

Sevda Greauvgiua (8)
St Michael's Primary School, Newry

Galaxy Moon

I woke up on a galaxy moon,
I have to go to bed soon.
Then I saw the sun,
I'd rather eat a bun.
Then I wanted to go to Saturn,
But Saturn was a big pattern.
My dreams are not going to stop me,
I'm gonna go drink some tea.

Ruby McVerry (7)
St Michael's Primary School, Newry

I Am A Teacher

I've always dreamed of becoming a teacher,
A teacher as smart as an owl,
As loud as a class,
As friendly as a smiling cat,
Singing songs,
Learning sums.

I hope my dreams come true!

Sophie Galbraith (7)
St Michael's Primary School, Newry

When

As I lie in bed,
My dreams fill my head,
Of one day becoming a face masher,
Being the best face masher,
Hard-working is paying off for money.

Nicole Hristova (8)
St Michael's Primary School, Newry

Once Upon A Dream Land

Where it's only sand,
And the rain is sand,
It is lonely,
It is hot,
There is no water,
There is nothing.

Lorcán Connolly (6)
St Michael's Primary School, Newry

The Realm Of Dreams

Those specks of light
Those wisps of smoke
These dreams fly through the air
They go to homes and houses and streets
To reach the children for whom they care

These specks of light
These wisps of smoke
Those dreams you know and love
They come from a land so far away
Where all those dreams are real

So come with me to this faraway place
It's weird and wonderful and true
It's wizards and knights
It's dragons all high
It's unicorns roaming the land
This wonderful place
This mythical world
It's known only as dreamland.

Basil Ransom (10)
Stockbridge Primary School, Edinburgh

Every Night, I Have A Dream

Every night, I have a dream.
Some happy, some funny, some sad.
But nothing has ever prepared me for this;
This swirling whirlpool of cruelty and dread.

For that night, I lay in bed.
The infrared beams switched off and on.
Then I stepped forward;
The wrong thing to do!
She stared at me.
And what happened next was from a horror movie.
She ran forward, grabbed me,
And in a flash I was her, leaning over me.

But then it was over, I was back on the ground.
She laughed, a grating high-pitched cackle.
Then, with a sword in the heart, I woke up sound.

Elsa Brett (10)
Stockbridge Primary School, Edinburgh

The Pirate Astronauts

Here in space we float around
We've got a massive ship which holds us down
Down at the bottom of the ship it holds all our rum
That we drink at eleven
We go around the moon
A ship growing all day
Our ship flies all around space just like a plane
Flying place to place
It's as cold as Antarctica
All the gas giants grumpy at night
Woah the pirate astronauts

The ship all wooden when you touch
You get splinters or nightmares
All over the ship you smell pirates' rum.
The pirates are happy
Then the ship disappeared.

Archie Roberts (10)
Stockbridge Primary School, Edinburgh

The Magic Of The Moon Is Like A Dream

Up above the clouds,
In amongst the stars,
That is where my moon realm dwells,
My castle in the sky,
Me, the Moon Princess, looking down at that crystalline sphere,
Earth,
Up in space, in my chest,
This is where my power shall rest,
Floating with the asteroids,
Travelling through the door of time,
Drifting through the voids,
There is a star,
Not just any star, but a star of hope,
Here I am,
On the moon,
Protecting the world from sudden doom,
Here in my dream world,
My palace is full of magic and wonder.

Freya Blathwayt (10)
Stockbridge Primary School, Edinburgh

Dreamland

Roses are red, violets are blue
This is Dreamland
And we are happy to have you.
Trees fly, fleas cry,
Dragons, fly in the bright sky.
Spiders scare
While dancers dare.
Vampires can't bear the sun near there.
Teachers teach while clowns are at the beach
Writers have to listen to the mayor's speech.
Footballers kick, tailors knit
While basketballers change their kit.
Fairies sigh, wizards tie while monsters lie.
Cows moo, witches boo
Mums vacuum while volcanos boom.

Emir Karabacak (10)
Stockbridge Primary School, Edinburgh

Nightmares

I am lost in a tower,
With no help in sight.
Until I see a bit of light,
I run as fast as a lightning strike,
But someone is chasing me on her bike.
When I get to the light, it disappears,
With a *whoosh* and a *bang*, she appears,
The tower jumps up,
She and I end up in a clump,
I see the exit, it is shining like the stars,
She scratches me, now I have a scar.
I managed to escape that dreadful tower,
It feels like it's been one hundred hours.

Jasmine Spence (11)
Stockbridge Primary School, Edinburgh

Nightmare

I sleep on my purple bed when I feel something
Crawling up my back
I feel frightened
So I scream but I can't
My mouth can't move
The room is as dark as night
I am as still as a pencil
I hear something pop
I try and see what it is
But I can't
I try to get up but something stops me
Suddenly, a giant spider jumps on me
Everything dances in the room
I can finally scream
I woke up but it was just a dream.

Maria Coelho-Spanos (10)
Stockbridge Primary School, Edinburgh

The Nightmare

A little girl down in the dust,
A deep dark forest covered in must.
A squirrel that played and laughed in the day,
A girl that cried and sang until dawn to dark.

A portal opened up one fateful day,
Frozen in fear like a ghost possessed her body.
She disappeared without a trace,
Nobody heard from the little girl since.

Some say she got stolen by a thing that took her soul
And took her life and they call it The Nightmare!

Ghofran Almutbage (10)
Stockbridge Primary School, Edinburgh

The Dream

When I go to bed and the clock goes tick-tock,
I hear a weird noise and the door begins to lock,
Then I hear a bang and a hat falls down,
But then I look up, there stands a clown!
His eyes are as red as lasers and he is as scary as a bat,
Then he starts to cackle and I fall down on the mat,
I land on his hat which is sharp and not flat,
Then I wake up and I am full of fear,
But then I realised it was all a dream
Oh dear!

Isla Gilchrist (11)
Stockbridge Primary School, Edinburgh

A Dream Is A Place

A dream is a place not a thing
You can't reach out and touch it
A dream is alive with a mind of its own
In a magical land far away
Where birds sing, trees swing
And grass is soft as a pillow
Where sun kisses your cheeks
And the heat sometimes peeks
As you drift away on your cloud of silvery blue
You'll think of Dreamland and it will think of you!

Elsie Douglas (10)
Stockbridge Primary School, Edinburgh

Dreams

Dreams are dreams, good or bad,
a dream could be a happy place,
Where you go to relax.
You could dream about
Birds, flowers, or even butterflies.

You could have a dream that
You don't remember, or you
Could have one that you'll never forget.
But it doesn't matter!
A dream is nobody else's,
It's just yours!

Thea McDougall (10)
Stockbridge Primary School, Edinburgh

Snowballs

There is a place called your imagination
A place where you have all your dreams
A place where you think about things that are not real
In your dream is a house
A house full of snowballs
One of the snowballs was sad
Another was happy
Another was angry
And another one was dancing all of his troubles away.

Albie Dagless (10)
Stockbridge Primary School, Edinburgh

Mythical Mermaid

M y tail gleams in the sun
E very day more and more fun
R ides with the playful dolphins in the sea
M y favourite place to be
A ll around me, blue and green
I t's the most beautiful thing I've ever seen
D reaming one day that's where I'll be.

Petra Kyriakides (10)
Stockbridge Primary School, Edinburgh

The Cloudy Dreamland

We're flying to dreamland, look around,
Clouds are all you can see.
Look below and you will see,
The magical world that we live in.
In Dreamland the clouds are as bouncy as a bed,
And the sky is as beautiful as a butterfly.
Anything that's possible in a dream,
Is possible in Dreamland.

Emile Henry-Davies (10)
Stockbridge Primary School, Edinburgh

My Warm Home

Naya is my name
I'm an aunt, yeah, I'm small
But I'm strong,
I love my house, oh I forgot to tell you
I have a flower house, it's pink,
Soft and smells amazing
It's like a marshmallow.
Every day, my friend would say hey
He is kind, happy and he is always there for me.

Naya Alzoubi (10)
Stockbridge Primary School, Edinburgh

Bat Sponge

As he flies through the night
As he strikes fear into enemies
As he fights crime
Villains fight the
Bat Sponge
As he saves the city
As Bikini Gotham thanks him
Bat Sponge flies away
As he hides away
As he sits in the sponge cave
As he hides his identity as
Sponge Wayne.

Andria Khupenia (10)
Stockbridge Primary School, Edinburgh

Nightmares

Nightmares, nightmares
They come to us all
Nightmares, nightmares
They make you feel small
Spiders, clowns and werewolves too,
Vampire bats that jump and go boo
Nightmares, nightmares
They make you scream
Then you wake up and it's all a dream.

Noah Sherwin (11)
Stockbridge Primary School, Edinburgh

Fire

I'm alone
No one to comfort me
I feel bitter and in pain
Everyone is gone
I'm in despair
The only light in my life is the fire burning my thoughts
All my memories destroyed
I'll never get them back.

Billie Morton Giovacchini (10)
Stockbridge Primary School, Edinburgh

Blossoming Dreams

As dawn rises on the land
Many shall rest for the break of dawn
As they rest
Many imaginations bloom vividly
All over with dreams swooping feral
All with a pinch of imagination
Anything is feasible in Dreamland.

James Lim Young (10)
Stockbridge Primary School, Edinburgh

In Some Sort Of Dream

Dreams, oh my dreams,
Can come in any shape,
Rays of shiny beams,
With a dazzling cape,
Can be weird and wacky,
Some in a funny way,
Some very scary,
In the sky so grey.

Diane Oreoluwa Afolabi-Fakunmoju (10)
Stockbridge Primary School, Edinburgh

The Unknown Festival

Unexpectedly, I got pulled underground by a skeleton hand.
I fell from a dangerous height but I got caught by a beautiful skeleton.
Dangling from a rope, patterned lanterns bobbed up and down.
Smashing a piñata, exploding candy burst out.
Cutting fruit like a cook with a sharp knife, the skeleton chopped the melon into a marigold.
Dangling on a rope across the scree, seven giant skeleton puppets danced to a good tune.
But suddenly, I woke up and realised it was all a dream.

Kyle (8)
Sutton Road Primary School, Mansfield

The Dream

Menacingly, a marigold came to life,
And wrapped its stem around my arm like a snake.
Deep, deep, deep into the depths
Of the grave, I fell.
A shaking, excited, happy skeleton played a guitar,
People dancing at the festival,
Dancing and singing skeletons,
People were eating.
Bouncing on a floating balloon,
I was scared,
My heart was beating fast,
My hand was trembling,
I opened my eyes,
It was a dream.

Freyja Wyatt (8)
Sutton Road Primary School, Mansfield

Dia De Los Mountas Nightmare

Suddenly, a sharp hand popped out of the ground and grabbed me on the arm. I was as scared as a mouse. I was walking backwards when a spooky, scary skeleton with a marigold touched me on the shoulder.

Being silent, weird, spooky graves were covered in orange marigolds.
The beautiful sound of the ukulele filled my ears.
The colourful piñata exploded in front of my eyes.
I fell out of bed with a loud bump!

Petros Murataj (9)
Sutton Road Primary School, Mansfield

Planet Zharkal

Never-ending darkness
I searched for a planet that
My gadget didn't mock us
As fascinating as a magician

There were enormous heroes
That were strong like a magnet.

Climbing higher and higher
Like I have never done before
My ears were filled with singing
Caroling and more.

I wander further
An acid stench fills my nose.

Then I started coughing up
Until an alien grabbed my arm.

Then I woke up in my bed
I wasn't very calm.

Teddy Butler (8)
Willows Primary School, Grimsby

Tank Nightmare

My ears filled with gunfire,
Explosions and deathly screams,
Enormous and extremely armoured tanks,
As powerful as a tsunami, crushed all in their path.
Sweat warmed my palms,
Fear ran through my body,
It smelt rancid, like an unwashed man,
Whoosh!
A missile soared through the air,
Drilling through the ominous clouds,
My heart froze,
My eyes opened.

Maxwell Leonard (7)
Willows Primary School, Grimsby

The Children Cursed Planet

It was as dark as a shadow
Where am I?
I explored and heard, "Oooooh!" in a ghastly moan.
It was as cold as Antarctica.
Where am I?
I smelt blood and flesh run up my leg.
The floor was as tough and as smooth
As human skin.
My mouth tasted blood and fear ran up my spine
And tasted toxic.
Where am I?
I open my eyes.

Emmanuel Ratubuli (7)
Willows Primary School, Grimsby

Fairytopia

Sparkles, as bright as diamonds, flash in my eyes.
Flapping wings echo in my ears
And gems clatter gently upon the Violet Hills.

The sweet scent dances in my nose
Like how candies delight me.

I gobble scrumptiously sweet cupcakes.
They taste like rainbows!

Tiny feet tickle my fingertips
As gentle as butterfly wings.

Amelia Kaminska (7)
Willows Primary School, Grimsby

Holiday Dreams

Splash,
Rain droplets soothe my burning skin,
Sunlight as bright as gods,
Beats down upon me,
Chlorine overpowers my nose,
The clean scent is almost acidic,
Sliding, slipping,
The smooth slide cushions my skin.

Joshua Evans (7)
Willows Primary School, Grimsby

Terrifying Squid

In the middle of the night
I hear crunch, crash from the beach.

Tentacles grab me by the shoulders
Terrified out of my skin.

Run, run, run
My brain screams at me.

Lucas Cottard (7)
Willows Primary School, Grimsby

The Happy Life

Disney is amazing,
Disney is magical,
Disney is colourful,
Disney is full of hamburgers,
Disney has a splendid castle,
Disney is where I want to live.

Alexander Williamson (7)
Willows Primary School, Grimsby

The Puma's Call

I love to play football
To show off my skills
Proud in the colours of my team
We all wear bright green.
We start the game with a centre kick
The ball goes flying *ever* so quick
Darting about in the rain, wind and snow,
Stopping when the ref's whistle does blow.
Aiming for the *net*
Keen for a goal and not to upset.
My team try sooo hard
But... oh no, what's that? A ref's card.
It's *red* for my friend...
The rules she did bend
And we are down to *ten*!
But wait, here's my chance
To make the fans dance.
Bang! I score a goal!

Nancy Carter (9)
Woodmancote School, Woodmancote

Daydream

In my daydream I fell into a potion,
It felt like I was swimming in an ocean.
In my daydream, I counted the sheep,
There were lots of them I wanted to keep.
In my daydream, I swam with turtles,
All of them were different types of purples.
In my daydream, I fell on a balloon,
But when I looked up, I was on the moon.
In my daydream, I saw Goldilocks and the three bears,
But I accidentally broke one of their chairs.
In my daydream, I went to the beach,
We got a couple of sweets each.
Now you know that daydreams are fun,
You might want to have one.

Verity-Iris Rowles (9)
Woodmancote School, Woodmancote

Star

When I dream at night,
I dream of being a star.
Having my fun flight
Drifting through the dark.

I meet Jupiter, Earth and Mars
Venus, Uranus, Neptune
They're all my family, I think,
Drifting through the dark.

I saw some cats wearing helmets
I saw some cats wearing suits
I saw some cats wearing boots
They waved as I went past.

When I wake up, my heart starts to pound
I think I'm in space
I'm in my warm bed
Not drifting through the dark.

Marley Williams (9)
Woodmancote School, Woodmancote

Imagination

I dream of a magical land
M y trees are blue and there is pink sand
A nimals are running in the sun
G iggling and having so much fun
I have chocolate every breakfast, lunch and dinner
N o one tells me off, that's a winner
A nd all my friends are there with me
T hey dance and we swim in the sea
I love my dreamland in the sky
O ne night I could fly
N ow it's time for bed... sweet dreams!

Evie Kirchner (8)
Woodmancote School, Woodmancote

I Fell Into A Cloud

Once upon a dream, I fell into a cloud
When I looked up, I was very proud.
There were animals, parks and ropes of many, please.
Then I realised, I was in a circus of glee.
So I sat down and watched the deadly trapeze and the graceful dancers
The graceful presentation.
After the amazing show, I sat down and relaxed.
At the max.
As I relaxed, I thought of how I was and about the calm around.
Then I faded away and closed my eyes.
Then opened again, I was in bed.

Lily Robinson-Kirk (8)
Woodmancote School, Woodmancote

Funny Dreams!

F lying in the sky tonight
U nicorns take flight
N o more spooky clowns
N or spiders creeping around
Y ou know how soon it can be

D reams coming alive and dancing with me
R inging the bells above
E verybody sees a dove!
A beautiful sight I see
M ermaids swimming with me!
S uddenly I wake up, it's ended but what's to come?

Zoey Pervaiz (9)
Woodmancote School, Woodmancote

Midnight

M y gosh, look at me
 I 'm staring out across the sea
D own I look into waters that flow
N ow I realise I'm not alone
 I find myself thinking, *is this right?*
"**G** o, run!" screams a voice in my head
H ow, I do not know, I feel myself sinking down below
T o find that I'm cosy, not wet, in my bed at midnight!

Ariyah Anderson (9)
Woodmancote School, Woodmancote

Environment

E ach night I go to bed,
N ot a thought will go away,
V isions in my head,
I am thinking every day,
R ubbish in the sea,
O rangutans are sad,
N ature is the key,
M elting ice is bad,
E nd this today,
N ow I try and get to sleep,
T hink of another way. The planet we must keep.

Ivy Graham (8)
Woodmancote School, Woodmancote

The Dance Of The Bones

I peek through the bushes as the skeletons dance,
They're dancing, prancing around the fire,
The fish they're eating just drops right out,
The next thing I know I'm joining in the fun,
As we're dancing and prancing we're having lots of fun,
We're dancing till morning, yet we're quite tired.

Alice Fleming (9)
Woodmancote School, Woodmancote

My Perfect Dream

Cows chill in the afternoon,
Balloons all shapes and sizes,
Cats continue to like bats,
There are witches with stitches,
Sweets that go tweet,
There is a cosy corner,
Pillows everywhere,
Soft blankets that waft you,
Now you know my perfect dream,
It is a magical place.

Lilly-May Dancey (9)
Woodmancote School, Woodmancote

Dreamland

In my dreams every night,
I see a problem I just can't fight,
There is a commotion in the ocean,
With a magical potion,
The cackling wizard,
Created a blizzard,
But he could not win,
So he threw his wand in the bin.

Grace Pearce (8)
Woodmancote School, Woodmancote

Young Writers Est. 1991

YOUNG WRITERS INFORMATION

We hope you have enjoyed reading this book – and that you will continue to in the coming years.

If you're a young writer who enjoys reading and creative writing, or the parent of an enthusiastic poet or story writer, do visit our website **www.youngwriters.co.uk**. Here you will find free competitions, workshops and games, as well as recommended reads, a poetry glossary and our blog.

If you would like to order further copies of this book, or any of our other titles, then please give us a call or visit **www.youngwriters.co.uk**.

Young Writers
Remus House
Coltsfoot Drive
Peterborough
PE2 9BF
(01733) 890066
info@youngwriters.co.uk

YoungWritersUK   YoungWritersCW
youngwriterscw   youngwriterscw